SHAROPOVA SHAHLO
KHAHRAMONOVNA

Scientific and Theoretical basics for developing Communicative Competence through teaching English to students in Technical Higher Education Institutions

(Monograph)

© Sharopova Shahlo Khahramonovna

Scientific and Theoretical basics for developing Communicative Competence through teaching English to students in Technical Higher Education Institutions

by: Sharopova Shahlo Khahramonovna

Edition: December '2024

Publisher:

Taemeer Publications LLC (Michigan, USA / Hyderabad, India)

ISBN 978-93-6908-321-3

© **Sharopova Shahlo Khahramonovna**

Book	:	Scientific and Theoretical basics for developing Communicative Competence through teaching English to students in Technical Higher Education Institutions
Author	:	Sharopova Shahlo Khahramonovna
Publisher	:	Taemeer Publications
Year	:	'2024
Pages	:	130
Title Design	:	*Taemeer Web Design*

Sharopova Sh.K. Scientific and theoretical basics for developing communicative competence through teaching English in technical higher education institutions: A Monograph / Sharopova Sh.K.

This monograph clarifies the scientific and theoretical foundations for developing communicative competence through teaching English in technical higher education institutions.

Reviewers:

Bukhara State Pedagogical Institute Professor, Doctor of Pedagogical Sciences (DSc) **G.V. Izbullaeva**

Bukhara Natural Resources Management Institute Associate Professor, (PhD) **N.I. Abdullayeva**

The monograph is prepared according to the standard English teaching method curriculum by the Ministry of Higher Education, Science, and Innovation of the Republic of Uzbekistan. signed and recommended by the Scientific Council of Bukhara Natural Resources Management Institute. (November, 2024)

CONTENTS

INTRODUCTION …5

System of competencies and communicative competence of engineering students …11

Modernization of higher education and development of students' communicative competence in English …36

Modeling professional competence based on teaching English for future engineers …64

Conclusions …95

References …101

INTRODUCTION

Worldwide, scientific research is being conducted on improving the theoretical foundations of training competitive engineering personnel in the process of integration in economic, social, and spiritual spheres, as well as developing the communicative competence of future engineers through teaching foreign languages using innovative educational technologies. Consequently, in the higher education systems of developed countries, including the USA, South Korea, Japan, and France, significant emphasis is placed on future specialists mastering multiple languages. It is considered crucial to focus on scientific research aimed at developing international cooperation in technical higher education institutions, enhancing the communicative competence of future specialists based on interdisciplinary integration of social-humanitarian, natural-scientific, general professional and specialized disciplines, studying the linguistic landscape of the world, and training highly qualified personnel in accordance with international standards.

Globally, numerous scientific studies are being conducted to develop students' communicative competence in English through the widespread use of mobile educational technologies and multimedia electronic learning complexes in the educational process. The rapid increase in international educational programs within the framework of the Bologna Convention also requires students to possess skills to use English not only from a professional standpoint but also as an academic field of communication. Teaching English to future engineers necessitates improving the methodology for developing communicative competence and its linguistic, sociocultural engineering, pragmatic, and strategic components, as well as cognitive and operational-technological professional competencies.

In our country, legal and regulatory foundations have been established to develop the communicative competence of engineering students based on foreign language teaching, organize educational content according to the Common European Framework of Reference (CEFR) international standards, and improve the quality of foreign language education by implementing international standards for assessing the quality of teaching. The Strategy of Actions for the Further Development of the Republic of Uzbekistan has identified priority areas for improving state youth policy, educating an intellectually and comprehensively developed young generation, enhancing the quality of education in higher education institutions by implementing international standards for assessing educational quality, and intensifying the teaching of foreign languages.

As a result, significant opportunities have been created to develop the communicative competence of engineering students in technical higher education institutions based on foreign language teaching. In this context, it is necessary to improve the content of foreign language teaching in technical universities in our country and to develop a methodology for existing pedagogical technologies and teaching methods.

The scientific and theoretical foundations for developing professional competence of future specialists in our country and enhancing language competencies of engineers have been elucidated in the research works of U.I. Inoyatov [56], R.H. Djuraev [45], J.J. Jalolov [47], D.M. Isroilova [58], N.A. Muslimov [86], A.A. Ashurov [20], F.A. Akhrorova [19], Y.T. Umarova [122], I.N. Ilkhomova [54], M.R. Kadirova [59], Kh.A.

Mamatkulov [77], K.D. Riskulova [101], Sh.K. Primov [98], and other scholars.

CIS scholars such as A.V. Khutorsky [128], T.S. Serova [110], Yu.G. Tatur [120], V.Yu. Frolov [124], G.V. Rogova [104], E.N. Solovov [108], G.P. Shchedrovitsky [136], L.S. Vygotsky [36], R.A. Kuznetsova [70], and others have scientifically and theoretically substantiated the issues of developing communicative competence in English for future engineers in technical higher education institutions, modernizing foreign language teaching, and evaluating foreign language proficiency indicators.

Foreign scholars including R. Jones [144], G. Dubbel [143], L. Malvern [145], P. Descy [143], M. Tessar [139], M. Rass [150], I. Schumpeter [141], I.L. Bimm [147], and others have conducted research on developing foreign language communicative competence of future engineers, and mastering operational knowledge and practical skills of written and oral communication in a foreign language.

The analysis of the conducted research reveals that information and communication technologies have not been sufficiently utilized in developing the language competence of future engineers. Furthermore, there is a lack of information and didactic support in foreign languages for general professional and specialized subjects, a low level of foreign language proficiency among students, and ineffective use of interactive teaching methods in the process of interdisciplinary foreign language instruction in combination with educational technologies and modern information and communication technologies. This underscores the urgency of improving the methodology for developing the communicative competence in English of future engineers.

System of competencies and communicative competence of engineering students

In the global education system, special attention is being paid to educating competent professionals in the field of engineering through teaching English to learners, developing the communicative competence of future engineers based on English language instruction. In technical higher education institutions, it is becoming increasingly important to organize the educational process in modules, modernize the English language teaching system through the application of innovative teaching methods, develop a methodology for teaching professionally-oriented English, and enhance communicative competencies in future engineers by implementing advanced methods of interdisciplinary English teaching in the educational process, making extensive use of modern information and pedagogical technologies.

To determine the system of competencies for future specialists studying in engineering fields, it is first necessary to consider the definition of the engineering profession. This definition is significant because it is based on examining the components and functions of engineering activities, which include production and technological, design, research, manufacturing and adjustment, organizational management, service, and other types of activities. Thus, in carrying out design activities, an engineer should possess the knowledge and skills to use standard automation and design tools in accordance with technical specifications, calculate and design components, develop technical projects and working documentation, register completed project work documents, monitor the compliance of developed projects and technical documentation with standards, technical conditions and other regulatory documents, conduct preliminary technical and economic studies of project calculations, and perform other related tasks.

In the qualification requirements for educational programs, engineering is described as a profession aimed at implementing and improving skills and abilities that are integrated with knowledge in the fields of mathematics, science and technology, business and management, and formed through specialized education and practical experience. The field of application for engineering is creating infrastructure and producing goods and services for state and industrial needs. An engineer's activity is intellectually based on the continuity of knowledge related to design, synthesis, and innovation. Engineering, as a professionally and socially significant activity, is defined as a set of important characteristics that are inextricably linked with the competencies acquired by graduates of technical higher education institutions.

Teaching subjects to students in the traditional way during the educational process is not sufficient for their effective learning. Methods of cognition and professional activity should be organically integrated. In this regard, the priority task of the engineering education system is to create sufficient conditions for the development of knowledge and professional activity culture in mathematical, natural science, general professional, specialized, and humanitarian disciplines.

One of the urgent tasks at various stages of higher education development in our country is to determine the theoretical and scientific foundations of the professional training process for students and to develop its professional program based on foreign language teaching. The initial research on studying and developing these issues through foreign language teaching in higher education institutions was conducted by prominent scholars in the field of pedagogy, such as J. Jalolov [47] and G.T. Makhkamova [79]. The principles of these scholars, based on connecting the training and education of future specialists with practice, are considered theoretically and practically leading.

According to J.J. Jalolov [48], G.T. Makhkamova [79], L.T. Akhmedova [20], G.Kh. Bakieva [23], and K.J. Riskulova [103], professional competence in foreign language learning is understood as an individual's readiness to apply acquired knowledge, skills, and experience in problem-solving. Competence is often viewed as a person's ability to perform certain professional functions. It is defined as an integrated characteristic of a person's personal and creative qualities, expressed through the set of knowledge, skills, and abilities manifested in the subject's personal activity, the future specialist's possession of relevant competence, the person's experience including their personal attitude and subject of activity, the ability to carry out any activity in specific professional situations, and readiness for action.

Based on the above analysis, competence requires constantly enriching one's knowledge, studying new information, sensing the demands of the times, mastering the skill of finding new knowledge, and applying it in practical activities. A specialist who possesses competence should be able to use methods and techniques appropriate to the specific situation in problem-solving, select and apply methods suitable for the current situation, reject inappropriate ones, and approach issues critically.

The most commonly used definition of

professional competence is that each person should have thorough knowledge of their work, and it is considered to encompass the essence of the work, phenomena and processes, complex relationships, its methods, means, and the nature of achieving intended goals. At the same time, competence requires the potential readiness to solve problems related to modern knowledge that includes the content of knowledge and skill components, and involves understanding the essence of the given problem and the ability to solve it.

Currently, the term competence is viewed as an integral part of professional skill. In solving these problems, it stimulates the self-awareness of future specialists as an essential indicator of professional development, a factor of self-analysis and development, and is characterized as follows: Professional competence is only influenced by the motives, goals, and intentions of real actors implemented in certain situations, and becomes part of competence along with personal abilities based on external requirements and the social context of the situation.

The concept of competence includes cognitive and non-cognitive components that can be mobilized for effective action, namely motor and mental skills, knowledge and moral orientations, social and behavioral components, actions arising in non-traditional teaching situations in higher education institutions, and through these actions, it is acquired and formed throughout life.

According to our analysis of the studied literature, the concept of "competence" is shown to refer to: processes and functions, mental actions, personal and positive qualities of an individual, motivational desires, values and orientations, practical skills, phenomena that equate intellectual, moral, social, aesthetic, and political aspects of knowledge.

In the current context, important features of professional competence cannot be considered separately, as they are integral and inseparable as a product of the entire professional training. Therefore, despite all the differences in approaches to professional competence, authors include communicative competence in it.

Using a competency-based approach to solve the tasks set in defining the purpose, direction, and content of higher education is considered one of the most effective methods. As a result, it helps to guide the personal development of education, creative initiative, student independence, competitiveness, and mobility of future engineers. N. Chomsky [127], R. White [150], J. Raven [102], and N.V. Kuzmina [71] have extensively studied the problems related to the competencies of future specialists in various aspects of higher education.

V.I. Baydenko explains competencies as "including knowledge, skills, abilities, and understanding, that is, theoretical knowledge of the academic field, the ability to know and understand, knowing how to act, the ability to apply knowledge practically and quickly in certain processes, and the ability to communicate with others in the social sphere." In his opinion, "competencies are a combination of characteristics that describe the degree to which a particular person is capable of implementing these competencies" [22].

Competencies are divided into professional and general professional types. V.I. Baydenko [22] proposes general competencies as competencies of social interaction, systemic-activity, self-organization and management, value-semantic and political-legal, and independent cognitive activity competencies.
When determining professional competencies,

attention is paid to the state educational standards for bachelors and masters in the field of engineering.

According to the classification under discussion, it is possible to conditionally include four competencies of social cooperation in the composition of intercultural-communicative competence in foreign languages. These are: knowledge of a second language, that is, the ability to express thoughts orally and in writing in several languages, as well as interpersonal relationship skills, namely understanding the culture and customs of other countries, accepting multiculturalism, the ability to work in diverse cultural environments, and the ability to communicate interculturally and work in an international environment.

The current state educational standard specifies the total and professional competencies that each graduate student in the technical field must possess. For example, it was noted that the direction of education 5450400-"Hydraulic Structures and Standards," adopted in 2020, should include 18 national competencies (UK) and 26 professional competencies (K) of graduates of the State Educational Standard for Higher Education in the field of training [14]. Among the four competencies mentioned above, the current standard actually includes requirements at the level of social and daily communication (UK-17) and tolerance to other cultures (UK-3). It should be noted that the system of competencies is dynamic.

According to K.E. Bezykladnikov[23], the relationship between professional competence and the presence of other competencies that manifest themselves in the quality of dialectical development in the sphere of activity is determined by the fact that there is a link between professional competence and other competencies that manifest themselves in the quality of dialectical development in the sphere of activity, that there is a link between the quality of professional competence and the quality of professional competence, that there is a link between the quality of professional competence and the quality of professional competence, that there is a link between

It has been established that the main goal of a competent approach is to shape a professionally socialized individual in terms of motivation, knowledge in the social, moral, and cultural spheres, as well as practical and technological aspects.

This competency shall answer the competency and shall include the following structural components:

a) motivation - readiness to demonstrate enhanced competence as an attraction of subjective qualities;

b) acquiring knowledge about the essence and content of cognitive competencies;

c) practitioners of competence in various types of processes;

g) value - the essence of competence and its relation to the object of application;

d) Emotional-moral treatment of the victim and demonstration of competence [23].

In I.A. Zimnyaya's research, competencies are defined as "knowledge-based, intellectual, active with personality, personal qualities and virtues, ethnocultural adaptability yields results" [47].

Competency is defined as the ability to express a person who possesses relevant competencies, a personal attitude towards work and activity, a "knowledge-based, intellectual, and social-positive personality." That is, if competence is a systemic, integrative quality of an individual, then we can consider competencies as elements of a system characterized by subjective, procedural, and other factors.

For our research, I.A. Zimnyaya's definition of "Communicative Competence" is of great importance, it is defined as "a very complex personal education, its existence and nature, characteristics of personality and personality, characteristics of personality." According to I.A. Zimnyaya, the components of communicative competence include the following:

1) methods, quotations, and processes of forming an opinion on the activities of the national community, the conditions of the state, or as a socio-cultural aspect of it;

2) language communicative abilities;

3) the conditions of speech activity; a value attitude towards science,

4) the emotional characterization of the culture of the individual as a component of the individual's personal agenda;

5) The readiness of the object for activity [50].

A.V. Khutorskiy,[128] Yu.G. Tatur,[129] V.Yu. Frolov,[129] and other researchers have expressed their views on the importance of developing students' competencies in educational practice.

T.C. Cerova identifies professionally-oriented English language instruction as subjective and does not align personal aspects with any competencies. It includes the following as the most important competencies:

1) mastering the skills of English communication, that is, speech;

2) multifaceted communication skills as a communicative-communicative interaction of exchange at the informational, emotive-multifaceted, analytical, and multifaceted levels;

3) proficiency in all types of speech activity in English;

4) models and skills of group and multi-group

collective relationships, the ability to work in a team;

5) Information in the socio-cultural and professional spheres within the framework of communication culture;

6) Thinking forms, mental operations and ways of forming thought, mnemonic processes and assignments;

7) English language lexicology - thesaurus;

8) socio-cultural processes and materials in the field of dialogue culture;

9) professional-oriented processes in the spleen.

10) personal qualities and individual abilities of social, cultural, professional orientation;

11) skills, skills, and abilities of a technician to create their own creative potential;

12) the ability to connect individual goals and goal outcomes to collective goals and outcomes;

The rapid technological, reflexive, and professional activity based on motivational values as a "support tool" in the implementation of the engineering model was encountered in the works of L.V. Mepkylova[82]. According to the classification, knowledge of foreign languages is included in the invariant component of professional competence, while skills are included in the organizational and technological component. When considering the goals of modern higher education and the path to achieving them, it is impossible not to take into account the significant changes in the content and essence of engineering professional activity that have occurred in recent years. The factors determining this are global changes such as the globalization of labor processes in the socio-cultural sphere, the possibility of using an international knowledge base, the use of information technologies, the development of methods for organizing professional activity based on the foundations of professional activity, the development of scientific and methodological foundations, and the development of methods for organizing professional activity. Accordingly, over the past decade, the number of basic professional competencies and components of training has increased. The following table outlines the content and essence of competencies.

table 1.1.1.

Engineering competences

Competences	Definition
Technical	Acquisition of knowledge and skills
	Knowledge of economics and professional disciplines
	Knowledge in fundamental sciences
	Mathematical thinking ability
Personal	Self-assessment
	Intersubject communicative ability
	Will and ability to learn
	Acceptance of international rights and regulations
Professional	Acceptance of high standards

	Personal accountability and ethnicity
	The ability to carry out professional activity in a non-standard setting.
	Use of professional communication in a foreign language
Management	The ability to master management skills and concepts
	The ability for work as a confidant
	Financial and technical management skills

It should be noted separately that a person possesses knowledge in a specific field, and it is determined that they can implement it, use it at an operational level in activities aimed at activity, and use equipment specific to the field of knowledge. The multiple use of knowledge acquired in the process of activity leads to the gradual formation of skills, the formation of the corresponding professional vocabulary. In this sense, acquiring knowledge and skills increases a person's activity, their readiness to perform professional activity.

According to the researcher, the ideas about the professional competencies of future engineers are widespread both in developed countries and in countries with a type of economy. The main reason for this is that, incidentally, all engineering companies are subject to various high-quality problems similar to the world economy.

Therefore, it is necessary to introduce a communicative component into the professional competence of foreign publications. According to the research, it can be said that if knowledge, skills, and abilities in the field of mathematical, natural-scientific, general professional, and technical sciences are the main content and essence of professional competence, then the study of a subject related to the social-scientific block can be considered multi-significant.

Mastering the operational-knowledge and

activity aspects of written and spoken English is considered the key to professional success in engineering. The development of a corresponding curriculum for improving students' communicative culture in the field of engineering and technology is organized by the American organization ABET-Accreditation Board of Engineering and Technology.

In preparing students for professional activity in the international labor market, they will be provided with an additional level of communicative competence in English. In studying the quality of modern engineering education, P. Jones emphasized the need for engineering education to enhance students' personal qualities that were not initially considered compulsory. To Bilap:

➢ Knowledge of the English language (at least one or two words in English and oral speech);

- knowledge of cultural characteristics of regions of the world where an engineer can operate in their field;
- knowledge of the fundamentals of international business (economic development, prosperity, international companies, etc.);
- Knowledge of technical aspects of engineering in international business (standards and standards, measurement systems, environmental regulations and regulations, etc.).

Pedagogical and psychological research and literary analysis show that in some regions of the world, the English language plays a critical role in terms of competence and employment. In India and China, there is a strong demand for graduates in the field of engineering, but most applicants find it difficult to find work. Due to this, both countries have a high unemployment rate among women with disabilities.

Basically, it is related to knowledge of the English language. According to many researchers, English "may open the door to the world of professional employment in India and abroad." Therefore, knowledge of the English language provides an opportunity for a graduate of an engineering university to freely engage in professional activity. Beyond the problems noted in China and India, there is a critical analysis of English language teaching, particularly the orientation of the educational process towards the knowledge paradigm of the relevant and promising competence paradigm.

The researcher's personal experience confirms the trend of cooperation with partners working with manufacturing, industrial, design organizations and engineering-oriented businesses. Working for candidates who can enter a full-fledged professional career in a foreign language is a good opportunity to meet the needs of the local population. Often, it is not so important for job applicants to know the language. However, taking into account the fact that the practice of face-to-face communication and video conferences is developing, it can be concluded that in the future, professional activity in the field of engineering will be improved in English with the ability to make an active professional communication, the ability to think in a flexible way and the ability to think in a positive way.

Modernization of higher education and development of students' communicative competence in English

American scholar F.G. Kimbs evaluates the unresolved problems of education as a crisis. "Depending on the conditions that have arisen in countries of this type, crises manifest themselves in a weak or mild appearance. However, the influence of y finds its reflection in a variety of countries that are renowned for their educational goals and do not repeat the call with great effort on the shy side" [72]. F.G. Kimbs, in his new work "Nazap after 80" after 20 years, writes about the educational crisis in the world, as well as about the fact that the overall process in the field of education is becoming more acute [72].

M.V. Bilanova emphasizes that the main task of the education system, which has caused a crisis in education, is not to put the creative character of society into the formation [32].

The emergence of an education crisis requires a change in the paradigm of education. A.D. Gonev[40], E.P. Belozentsev[25], A.G. Pashkov[93] in their research, consistently changing the paradigm of education based on an information-pedagogical approach, scientifically substantiated the idea of transforming the paradigm of education based on a holistic, comprehensive educational approach.

The perfection of the knowledge base is explained by the individual's ability to perfect relationships between nature, society, and themselves. D. Blanket, in response to the global challenge of the present day, proposes a transition to a comprehensive approach to the education system and close cooperation with the field of knowledge being prepared specifically [26].

P. Disse and M. Tesar's research focused on the implementation of didactic innovations related to the renewal of knowledge acquired in the course of human life, the differentiation and individualization of the educational process, and the improvement of the quality of teaching agriculture in the future.

Modernization of education is linked to the problem of increasing the effectiveness of education, responding to changing societal needs in a timely manner. This process can only be implemented through the development of individual competencies in students [132].

When we analyzed the word "modernization" etymologically and linguistically, it can be seen that it is derived from the English word "modern" and means "connected" or "corresponding to the present time" in the texture.9 Many of us believe that it is possible to create a typical style, that is, to introduce a new idea, idea or concept, to create a new style, to create a new style, to create a new style.

"Modernization" - modernization in accordance with the demands of the time, a change that includes various types of changes. Therefore, in modernizing education, we want to renew in accordance with the needs of the current generation. Modernization of higher education, based on its availability and quality, shall be based on the following modern progressive principles:

- ✓ Globalization: the rapid development of the global economy requires the migration of individuals across national borders, principles, and paradigms. These aspects require an enterprising, creative worker who strives to meet the set requirements.
- ✓ A cultural transformation of society, where one side uses audiovisual technologies (internet, television, radio), globalization and internationalization of the economy, and the other side, the introduction of an English-style

international project, the formation of a culture of self-awareness in one side.

✓ To recognize that education is the main source of perfecting the world, nature, and interpersonal relationships of the individual.

As a result of the organic implementation of the aforementioned principles, it is considered one of the most important conditions for the successful implementation of the process of education modernization.

According to E.N. Kolova, the development of the education system is characterized by the following:

To clarify the need for education throughout life based on the principle of 1."well-educated throughout life."
2. Transition from subordination to initiative.
3. Transition from education to competencies.

The main feature of updating education in the field of foreign language learning is..."locating its reflection in ensuring the organic connection of linguistic readiness with social-verbal, informational, pedagogical readiness."

The crisis in higher education is reflected in the fact that employers are not satisfied with the level of training. When preparing such a textbook, the Concept for Updating State Educational Standards shall be taken into account on the basis of the principles existing in higher education, namely:

Modernization of higher education can be understood as the process of interaction with the direct professional production of a higher educational institution. This, firstly, provides an opportunity to significantly expand information sources, and secondly, to enhance financing sources. Moreover, it will allow the student to undergo an internship in the databases and laboratories of leading companies, as well as to study for a long time in a foreign higher educational institution.

The humanization of higher education is the assessment of the cultural and intellectual level of the student, the social consequences of their activity, and the prevention of the consequences of their social activity (the main goal is to develop philosophical and economic readiness, active participation in the social and cultural life of society).

Knowledge of foreign languages and teaching and learning.

Taking into account modern market relations, it is necessary to eliminate the need for labor standards [131].

The effectiveness of future engineers is determined by the need to change the content and essence of education and include in the training process managerial, entrepreneurial, customer-oriented work, ensuring the quality of service, the quality of education, the quality of education, and the quality of education. The higher educational institution intends to reduce environmental education in the educational process.

M. Pace presents his point of view on the modernization of education. Moreover, modernization is aimed at introducing the best models that belong to the layer of culture, which characterizes the change in "modernization" and "reform," the role of the teacher in education, the essence of composition, structure and "development" [99].

Modernization of education is the task of transforming the world into the image of "the world as a subject" in the process of cultural-historical and social development. The task of transforming the world into the image of "the world as a human being" is to reveal the essence of the type, its constant development and development in the modern world. In this case, the value of product and even production technologies is not, on the contrary, the value of thinking: "A competent person in the field of science" is a person who is "living in knowledge," but a person who is a new person, an idea, a person who has a good sense of the world.

Another characteristic of social processes is the condition of interdependence and interdependence of the following aspects, which leads to a significant decrease in the responsibility of the changing entity and the opposing entity.

In our country, the modern education system is considered mandatory to answer the following challenge:

1. If it is unclear under what conditions a student lives and works, how can he be educated?

2. What kind of experience can be exchanged with it? Practice is the execution of actions of a typical type, the state in which the person previously acquired and applied the action in a specific process.

The objects of society and the processes of production change frequently. Such an interpretation of the existing process requires individuals to possess innovative abilities that allow them to be "ready for everything." Conceptual answers to the above-mentioned questions require the introduction of changes in the education system, and the ability to acquire ready-made knowledge, as well as the ability to adapt to changes in the subject, but also the ability to develop knowledge, if necessary, to implement changes in the subject.

Based on the needs of the labor market, in addition to the education system, there are "institutions for the development of qualifications and retraining of specialists, a company educational network, a multidisciplinary higher educational institution, a system for training personnel within the institution." This practice is mainly implemented in many developed countries with state programs on a foreign language (which found its logical reflection under the slogan "Butyn improvement throughout life"). All bills provide the opportunity to effectively communicate in one's workplace through the use of resources, materials, and resources.

While the presence of a system of skills development, such as a bra, increases the effectiveness of interaction between the modern labor market and the higher education system. In this case, the value of an individual is determined by the category of values accepted in an indigenous society. Therefore, it is important that the goal of education in an indigenous society is determined by "fast adaptation" of the individual to the work of a particular category.

In G. Tapd's research, "the driving force of societal development is a modernizing change and innovation, while research is a fundamentally new approach, and innovation is the assimilation of discoveries as a social and cultural norm." At the same time, the essence of modernization lies in the fact that its content lies not only in adapting to the needs of the individual and society and meeting the needs of the individual, but also in the leader of the individual, in the change of innovation in terms of quality.

In his works, M.A. Mozheiko argued that "the concept of modernization is a meaningful aspect of the concept of individualization, in particular, the essence of the content of an indigenous society is determined by the point of view of the intellectual and cultural transformation of the intellectual and cultural transformation, the essence of the transformation of the indigenous society."

Austrian economist I. Schumpeter, having separately demonstrated the unique mechanism of innovation implementation, promoted modernization, as well as in his research "science

- research - development - production," emphasized the effectiveness of self-development activity in the optics of self-development and self-development, as well as the effectiveness of self-development and self-development.

Currently, a significant portion of pedagogical theory has been studied, which is closely linked to the study of the least developed and separate aspects of the modernization of education.

Modernization of education is not only a sign of a systemic change in the quality of speech in the process of innovation, but also embodies the most effective directions for developing the internal potential of education.

We will consider the concept of modernizing the approach and practice of promoting and managing various socio-economic entities with objective laws and the possibility of promoting.

Modernization of the process of foreign language learning depends not only on innovation and innovation itself, but also on the implementation of only a part of the modernization process. The process of teaching a foreign language has changed not only in accordance with the demands of the time, but also in connection with other periods of the past, specifically:

1) A.A.Mirolyubov, A.V.Papaxina, A.Ya.Gaycina, L.I.Devina, M.G.Kochneva, I.V.Camoevich, N.D.Coloeva, C.A.Tilkina analyzed foreign language teaching in higher educational institutions, its role in preparing students for professional and professional training in the works of A.A.Mipolyubov, A.Ya.Gaycina, L.I.Devina, M.G.Kochneva

In the 50-80s of the 20th century, the problems of teaching foreign languages in non-philological higher educational institutions, the preparation of future teachers for professional activity were studied in the works of V.M.

Khalova, C.K. Flookan, I.M. Bemba, P.A. Knyazeva, L.V. Shilka, and others.

A.A. Miro Lyubov emphasizes that "mastering new methods and means of writing and receiving information in relation to one's native language can be one of the tasks of foreign language teaching." Practical mastery of a foreign language involves the practical mastery of both "oral" (listening and speaking), and "written language" (reading and writing).

This period is explained by the practical orientation of foreign language teaching, which involves reading at home, typing texts, and speaking. Due to the difficulties in teaching reading texts published in a foreign language, searching for a request, and the high level of confidentiality of all information, there is a lack of communication with international scientific and technical information.

In the curriculum of non-philological

educational programs in higher educational institutions, a small number of students are required to study a foreign language in the first year of foreign language instruction. The document proposes to continue the facultative training of the applicant in the first and fourth stages, dividing it into the ability to consciously study literature on the possibility of working in the field of employment, employment, graduation work, or the protection of employment in English.

In the 80th anniversary of the last century, the curriculum for a foreign language was developed by non-linguistic higher educational institutions based on the introduction of knowledge and abilities acquired by students in secondary schools to a standard level of speech, as well as the introduction of a comprehensive content-based approach to the development of skills and abilities of students in a mobile language.

The demand for oral speech includes teaching less complex conversations and listening to a complex topic. The essence of oral and written speech is not professionally oriented, on the contrary, it is based on socio-political, environmental, and general material.

2) From the 1990s to 2000, significant changes began to occur in the practice of teaching a foreign language to students of non-linguistic higher educational institutions. A non-linguistic university has begun to exert its influence on the target and content elements of foreign language instruction for students. During this period, a number of changes occurred in the paradigm of pedagogy. The humanization of training in a higher educational institution, student-centered learning, has begun to take off. The practice of teaching a foreign language, due to its novelty, new teaching methods, the scale of attracting foreign practice, and the fact that the country's

legislation and practice have already been introduced into the educational process of non-linguistic higher educational institutions, has a positive impact on the effectiveness of the educational process.

3) In 2000, at the latest stage, a high-quality environment began to emerge in the field of educational services in our country and foreign higher educational institutions. Bay has increased his attention to teaching foreign languages. English language instruction in technical universities has begun to be implemented in all classes. However, by 2017, the amount of training was reduced due to the fact that it did not reach the required level, and it began to be taught only in the first class. This is explained by the fact that learning English depends on learning how to work on one's own.

Integration and differentiation - "the relationship between one unit is dialectical, and the relationship between parts of one unit is analogous to the relationship between parts of one element, that is, it has unity: to combine, to restore unity." It is necessary to include a lot of explanations of these changes in one layer of causation.

First of all, professional competence in a foreign language is largely integrative. They integrate professional and foreign language training, competencies, and competencies.

Secondly, we will examine the professional competence of the English language in the context of professional activity in engineering, as the ultimate result of a person's integrity and pedagogical activity, as well as the role of a person in the formation of a competence that requires a synthetic analysis and a comprehensive analysis of the subject. His abilities are reflected in his productivity, in the realization of the opportunities available to him. Solving new problems requires analytical, synthetic, and reflexive abilities. It encompasses many aspects of self-organized pedagogical activity, "in ensuring self-organization in a way that differs from interconnectedness, it combines knowledge in various disciplines and introduces a new theory." M.N. Bespalova emphasizes that the essence and content of education are at the level of membership, which implies five levels of systematic approach-point-oriented integration [26].

The first level is an empirical level of the essence and content of education, focusing on the well-known principles of improvement from the point of view of higher education orientation and the laws of the modern paradigm of education.

The second level is the level of academic science, which at this level finds its reflection in the integrative politics of shaping the complex of personal competencies in the system of smooth development of the academic discipline "foreign language." The organic nature of foreign language learning is considered the basis for shaping the social and humanitarian culture of the individual, forming the main system for developing the competence of teachers based on English language instruction.

The third level is the level of academic material, which depends on the selection of academic material at this level and the formation of an organic attitude towards the relationship between academic material and work forms, leading to the elimination of boundaries in the academic discipline.

The fourth level is the level of readiness for professional activity in engineering.

The fifth level is the structural alignment of the future engineer-teacher's personalities, mutually influencing and changing in the process of their development.

Regarding the first level of the organic nature of the content and essence of education, it should be noted that foreign language instruction in technical universities is carried out in accordance with the State Educational Standards (State Educational Standards) of the educational directions and the requirements of qualification requirements (ST) and the requirements of foreign language instruction. The content and essence of the academic discipline related to teaching a foreign language in a modern higher educational institution are clearly defined by foreign principles, which require a standard approach to teaching a foreign language, a practical approach.

The need for widespread use of advanced foreign experience in foreign language teaching has always been high. It should be noted separately that the practice of teaching a foreign language has the essential content and practical experience of modernizing higher education. If the task of ensuring the coherence of teaching other academic subjects in the present day is emphasized or criticized, integration, like in the field of foreign language teaching, remains a natural task.

Modern methods of teaching English as a foreign language have gained widespread popularity, taking into account the modernization of language education in European countries, as well as the structural structure of the teaching process: the effectiveness of teaching English as a foreign language, the ability to acquire language, social and cultural competence, as well as the ability to protect elementary knowledge; the effectiveness of teaching English as a foreign language, the effectiveness of teaching English as a foreign language, the effectiveness of teaching English as a foreign language, the effectiveness of teaching English as a foreign

A weak feature of the proposed teaching

materials for the organization of high-quality education is that they consistently include visual, audio-video materials, teaching materials related to the independent conduct of educational activities, teaching materials related to the independent conduct of educational activities, teaching materials related to the content of the content of the content of the content of the content of the content of the content of the content of the content of the content of the content of the content of the content of the content.

Our research aims to implement a comparative study on the distribution of English language learning goals, presented in Table 1.2.1, currently accepted in leading foreign countries.

Changes and innovations in the education system are linked to the daily routine of the state and society. In the process of teaching a foreign language, it is important to answer the following question: "What and with what goal are we learning? Is language a product of intercultural cooperation or a scientific innovation?

Is it a language that is necessary for migration?" It is precisely in this way that the pedagogy of other countries also arises. In the education system, the diversity of national identity is observed, the provision of higher education is a responsible task of the nation and the state, and, first and foremost, its national conditions, stable tasks and limits are determined.

table 1.2.1.
A system for classifying foreign language learning goals for foreign countries.

Foreign classification system	Accepted classification system
1. EGP - English for general purpose	Teaching future engineers the basic aspects of language
2. ESP - English for specific purposes.	Teaching English to a non-philologist based on the direction of their professional activity

3. EST - English for scientific and technological purposes.	Teaching English for scientific research
4. EAP - English for academic purposes	English language instruction is approximated by the assignment of a certificate to students who plan to continue their education abroad
5. ESL - English as a second language.	English language instruction in English-speaking countries.
6. EFL - English as a foreign language	The applicant who studies a foreign language and does not have a state language in the country where he lives

The amount of foreign language instruction is characterized by the fact that technical education of this type is differentiated or mass education is provided.

The process of education modernization is

interconnected with the implementation of a competency-based approach to education and the implementation of a competency-based approach as the achievable outcome of the educational process.

In this process, special importance is attached to the formation of competencies, which implies a transition to a meaningful result achieved by the academic discipline. In addition to paying special attention to the skills of a competent approach, it is necessary to determine the effectiveness.

The capabilities of a foreign language subject should meet the following requirements:

1) rapid student adaptation;

2) To direct graduates to the development of full-fledged professional activity in the future according to the "development - world" criterion;

3) Compilation of State Educational Standards with a Comprehensive Structure of the European Education Classification [31];

4) the introduction of a new criterion in the practice of collecting a unit of tests (credit), which includes the teaching of certification procedures in the educational process;

5) to reduce the focus on analyzing the achievements of applicants and graduates, to demonstrate the level of their knowledge in the order of evaluation tools and technologies provided by a competent approach;

6) Increasing the level of demand for the choice of individual educational areas.

In conclusion, it should be noted that the competency-based approach involves not only ensuring compliance with the requirements set by the employee, but also ensuring the effectiveness of determining the qualitative qualities of the employee's ability to meet the requirements set by the employee, as well as improving the quality of the employee's ability to meet the requirements set by the employee.

Modeling professional competence based on teaching English for future engineers

Professional development and humanization are considered the main didactic directions of the social determination of the process of higher education. This is divided into two parts of the social requirement for an individual, namely the requirement for future production and the requirement for moral and spiritual development. Solving complex contradictions defines the main task of higher education in the present period. The main goal of higher education is the uninterrupted intellectual and professional development of a new type of education, and the following expression is used:

• a high level of international responsibility and social activity;

• knowledge, spiritual and cultural, motivation and skills to work with spirits;

• a high level of professional skills, innovative directions of scientific and technical thinking, the creation of new values and the adoption of a creative horizon;

• continuous self-education and new preparation;

• physical and mental health, professional ability to work.

Many studies conducted by our current educators are dedicated to researching the didactic direction related to the development of higher education. The aforementioned research defines the essence and content of higher education, based on the model and block diagrams presented in Table 1.3.

Table 1.3.1

The content of higher education

Cultural block	Psychological block	Science block

- methodological; - axiological; - socio-economic; - historical and cultural, communicative - natural science;	- guide; -theoretical methodological; - activity-based	- related to general, scientific knowledge; - an integrated, scientifically oriented applicant; - special

In modeling communicative competence in English, global and European principles of higher education development should be based on global principles, and higher education development should be based on global principles.

- broad classification of type, variety, multivariance and multi-model;

- the availability and academic independence of a single level of employment with a reduction in the accountability of higher education institutions;

- radical renewal and transformation of the higher education system, prior knowledge of the evolution of consumerism, constant adaptation of educational programs to future needs;

- strengthening other stages and forms of education, increasing the purposefulness of higher education;

- the transition of the higher education paradigm to the paradigm of life-long learning;

- giving the applicant the opportunity to choose the optimal scale of the competition;

- the ability to quickly adapt to the "starting" and "beginning" of obtaining higher information;

- to reduce the level of higher education in the formation of students' readiness to change, interpret, express and promote national, regional, international and traditional culture in connection with the diversity of the culture;

- upbringing of the applicant in the

international community and implementation of the applicant's orientation towards active participation in the life of society;

- the formation of special opportunities and strategies for the development of social leadership in higher education, the expansion of the relationship between higher education and production;

- achieving a level playing field in cognitive mastery of academic subjects and the acquisition of skills in the field of communication, creative and critical analysis;

- an increase in the focus on curricula within the framework of interdisciplinary and academic disciplines;

- the emergence of a new educational field based on modern technologies and a model for increasing educational services;

- the introduction of a model curriculum as a new organizational framework for teaching and learning, as well as the implementation of state standards for teaching the essence and content of modern higher education to the new generation.

The higher education system, being an external, internalized system in relation to the individual, "transfers" the internal process of their development in the process of mastering cultural values by the individual. The social culture of the media is inextricably linked to the professional culture of the media. At the level of professional culture, we strive to realize the creative potential of our national personality, aimed at mastering and implementing various types of activity and new scientific and technical knowledge, values, and technologies.

The professional culture of Metahaccis includes the following components:

- technological;
- axiological;
- personal-creative.

The process of mastering the essence and content of higher education takes the form of reflecting the characteristics and methods of professional activity of the student, the norms of culture in mastering the path of creation and research.

The mastery of the main block of the content and essence of higher technical education - general culture, psychology, and academic disciplines - serves as an external boundary in relation to the teaching of foreign languages in a higher educational institution.

The formation and development of communicative competence in English among students of technical universities, the formation of communication skills in the socio-cultural process, and the study of foreign languages are being implemented in a comprehensive manner. The technological model of communicative competence of future engineers in English, developed by us, takes into account all the most relevant factors and ensures their determination.

The subject "Foreign Language," which is considered the primary element of higher education, should contribute to the achieved result.

The main goal of foreign language teaching is to define a criterion from a social and pedagogical point of view. This, in turn, determines all other aspects of the organization. The content and essence of education, its references, principles, methods, organization and results, the content and essence of foreign language teaching in a higher educational institution are examined in the process of forming a demand for participation in professional and personal communication at the international and intercultural levels. Undoubtedly, the outcome of foreign language instruction is the ability and readiness to enhance intercultural interaction with representatives of other linguistic cultures belonging to a specific or borderline professional field.

We will consider the formation of communicative competence in English as the achieved result of the upbringing and formation of the future engineer's personality. As the goal of foreign language learning, we highlight three aspects: cognitive, pragmatic, and pedagogical [54]. Based on the nature of higher education, we propose changes to these aspects and reflect them in the following table.

**table 1.3.2.
The goal and main aspects of teaching foreign language**

Cognitive aspect	Pragmatic aspect	Pedagogical aspect
Thinking and understanding, reflexivity, interpretation, reflected in the	This is related to the practical use of extraneous means in	This is related to the development of the following qualities of a

| content of teaching English to students, are related to the culture of another people, revealing the values of the country where the language is being studied. | intercultural professional interaction, the development of skills in implementing large-scale professional interaction among students, and the further use of this method in the formation of their potential. | student: openness, initiative, tolerance, readiness for intercultural communication, independence, and creativity. The ability to change national mentality. The need to study and acquire knowledge. |

In each aspect, the essence of education corresponds to the essence of education, and it forms competencies at the beginning, and then competencies on the basis.

The content and essence of foreign language instruction in a technical higher educational institution are determined by the goal of our pedagogical approach, which, in turn, is linked to the goal of education. There are several approaches to defining the content and essence of foreign language teaching. N.D. Galskova[38] and N.I. Gaz[40] emphasize two aspects: subject and subject. The first is knowledge that is attracted for oral or written communication, the second is dependence on skills and learning. I.L.Bim[27], E.I.Passov[91] add knowledge about the world to the essence of foreign language teaching, the practice of implementing types of activity, as well as the experience of personal attitude to various objects.

Our research is close to the views of E.N. Solovova[10] and G.V. Rogova[11], who use three main linguistic, psychological, and methodological elements in foreign language teaching. Each of these elements forms the foundation of foreign language instruction for students in higher education institutions. He will also contribute to the formation of students' communicative competence in English in the future.

The interrelation of content and functional characteristics of content in foreign language teaching are presented in Table 1.3.

Table 1.3.3.

The essence of foreign language teaching and its elements

Linguistic element	Psychological element	Style - epistemological element
It does not encompass the literal material. Language is always subjective, processual, language is objective, and performs two functions: communicative and implicative	The language being studied by students includes skills and abilities that allow them to use it during their studies	Knowledge of innovations is linked to the development of skills in independent and academic work

To shape the communicative competence of future engineers in English, it is necessary to take into account one important factor in determining the essence of education:

1. Personal factor. That is, the growing importance of the personal factor in all spheres of activity underscores the importance of a new, anthropocentric approach to the study of any subject [34].

2. Combining scientific and technological progress with the ideas of humanism.

Knowledge of a foreign language is a key factor in the professional growth of future engineers and their socialization.

4. The introduction of technological thinking features into existing English language textbooks for technical universities.

5. The age-appropriate factor of student characteristics. It is precisely this that is the

factual aspect of knowledge, ensuring its dependence on the information and content of educational materials.

6. The factor of the intensity of socio-economic development in our country.

7. The global factor that implies the need to ensure communication with universal values, ideas, and cultures.

One of the main tasks of organizing the essence of education is to bring the professional and social orientations of students to a close balance. It is necessary to choose such a content-essence of education that it is suitable for the preparation of educational materials, at the same time for the general cultural needs of the individual and society. In accordance with the goals of education and the essence of teaching, we achieve the following group of competencies and evaluate them as a result of the educational process.

1. Cognitive competence related to acquiring knowledge, skills, and abilities in the field of English.

2. Pragmatic-communicative competence, "Do the world - know." Acquisition of knowledge and skills developed in the field of "English Language" and "Foreign Culture" in the field of professional and technical activity.

Communicative competencies are divided into:

- ➢ discrepant - as the ability to interpret texts related to each other.
- ➢ to have the ability to create linguistic and grammatical forms and use syntactic devices based on the linguistic criteria.
- ➢ socio-linguistic - the linguistic form and way of expressing it in language, the compatibility of the communication process with the terms, that is, the process of communication, its purpose and direction, the compatibility of chapters on

communication with the social and functional relationship.
- ➢ social culture - mastering the scientific and cultural characteristics of the country whose language is being studied by students.
- ➢ social - the ability to engage in practical communication and continue it.
- ➢ strategic - knowledge of the language, ability to compensate for the lack of speech and social experience.

3. Empathetic competence, or the individual's experience in assisting in an emotional-evaluative approach to linguacultural influence.

4. Gnoseological competence. "I don't know what to do next." It depends on thinking and understanding, interpretation, and the ability to attract the student to the English language and the culture of another people - a language carrier.

To develop a model for the formation of

communicative competence in English for future engineers, the "Tuning" curriculum, developed within the framework of international curricula, was analyzed, as well as the effectiveness of the effectiveness of the educational process in Europe, the effectiveness of the effectiveness of the educational process, First, social-personal, economic, and national competencies, then organizational-managerial, professional, and professional competencies. We have analyzed the structural structure of our universities, disciplines reflecting the specifics of the field, and academic disciplines-specialized competencies [134].

An analysis of the proposed competencies was conducted to determine the proportionality of competencies, readiness for knowledge on all sides, the possibility of developing innovative competencies, and the ability to use existing competencies in the future.

The proposed model of English language

teaching is primarily based on the "language aspect," which is considered relevant during the period of advancement in primary linguistics.

The general education system includes six interconnected and integral systems of English language proficiency:

- ✓ Breakthrough (level of living);
- ✓ Waystage (average calculated level);
- ✓ Threshold (middle level);
- ✓ Vantage (average stroke level);
- ✓ Effectiveness (high level);
- ✓ Mastery (level of language proficiency).

Given that a high level reflects the level of foreign language proficiency, it cannot be accepted as a model of non-verbal education in foreign language teaching for academic purposes, but can be supplemented with its content, used. The technical expert assesses the readiness of a professionally skilled applicant for engineering activity.

The obtained results of academic and cognitive activity in teaching English to students of technical universities include the formation of a communicative thinking, as well as cognitive activity and professional competence.

English language learning is aimed at mastering all the main functions of communication: cognitive, persuasive, value-oriented, as well as rules of etiquette. B.A. Lapidus, criticizing the process in the field of foreign language teaching, argues that "the development of a complex based on the skill of speaking, factual and easily acquired learning materials (linguistics, linguistics, etc.) and the development of practical skills reflecting the basic requirements of the content of the educational process" is an important task. This refers to the need for a significant increase in the number of practical exercises in English to shape the personality of a teacher in the future [73].

Almost 80 percent of school graduates are forced to "re-train" in higher education institutions due to their lack of English language proficiency.

Below is a diagram of the technological model, which includes blocks, models, conditions, and mechanisms that lead us to unlimited results based on factors that model the professional competence of engineering students in English language instruction.

table 1.3.4

Technological model for the formation of professional competence in foreign language for future engineers

The aim of pedagogical process is to develop the professional competence of technical specialists in a foreign language		
General block	Psychological block	Technological block
Educational modules Actions, communicative, personal-creative, historical-cultural, methodological, natural-scientific, practical-		

oriented		
Interactive	**Subject-active**	**Informative**
Psychological and Pedagogical conditions		
Formation mechanisms		
value orientation of competencies	Personal development in academic and professional activities, independent education, and self-expression	Emotional self-regulation of the formation and development of professional-personal-reflective competencies	Project-oriented activity of the teacher and students	Competence is a person's readiness to demonstrate themselves in a new way
Criteria and quantities		
Condition criteria	The aims, content, methods, and	The level of compliance with the chosen goal		

	means of education, age-related and individual characteristics of students	is: The formation of the "Men-ideal" in professional competence
Outcome criterion	Competencies - knowledge and skills	Linguistic, psychological, methodological, empirical
Readiness criteria	Competence	Levels (I–IV)
Level of formation of professional competence of technical specialists in a foreign language (result)		
I	Fixation	
II	Implementation	
III	Development	
IV	Research (creation)	

As the table shows, the achievement of the goal is based on three blocks, such as intercultural, psychological, and technological.

The content and essence of education are divided into axiological, communicative, personal-creative, historical-cultural, stylistic, natural-scientific, and practical educational modules. Interactive, subjective, and informational-pedagogical technologies were used to achieve the goal. The mechanism for shaping psychological and pedagogical skills, the criteria and shortcomings for shaping competence, and its levels are increasing.

To determine the characteristics of the criteria for the knowledge of professional foreign languages by specialists with higher technical qualifications, we classified professional English language competence from the Butyn system of classification as a standard. Therefore, in order to study the concept of work ethic, we rely on a system of criteria based on the following principles: the principle of education and self-education;

Professional competence in English is the ability of an experienced and reflective person to master the existing English language, professional intercultural communication, and methods of managing relationships with the goal of self-improvement and self-improvement in the process of professional development and self-improvement in the higher education system. It includes intercultural competencies, and at the same time, intercultural competencies.

It should be noted that intercultural competence (IC) primarily encompasses the ontological aspect of personality formation, while communicative competence encompasses the language and speech skills of the latter. It has been concluded that mutual complementation of intercultural and communicative competencies and mutual influence of individual competencies can be formed in detail.

Researcher O.V. Siromyasov believes that

cross-cultural communication and intercultural competencies cannot be successfully implemented without understanding the national worldview and the effectiveness of communication.

The need to satisfy the spiritual needs of students is unnecessary, and at the same time, the production and economic functions of education are not fully realized. The response to the social need for professional development and humanization of education, the orientation of the individual, increases the accurate orientation of education towards the general cultural and humanistic function. Our surveys conducted over the years have shown that the socio-cultural process increases the impact of students on assessing the humanistic function of education. Therefore, one of the main tasks of organizing the content of education is to harmonize the professional and humanitarian orientations of students, to form the readiness of students to develop their professional activity in general, specifically, intercultural communication.

They solved one of the common results of the data processing process. The story begins with a description of the myth. The second step is to evaluate the components of the problem to determine the need for information and the need to solve a specific task. The third step is to pre-evaluate the list of medications and supplies. To choose the most optimal one, try to know the influence or consequences of each agent in advance. The ability of an intellectually developed person to receive information about one of their characteristics.

The criterion for future engineer's knowledge of English is the definition of goals related to the future professional activity of the engineer. We are achieving these goals at three levels. The first level of goals is the novelty, consistency, accuracy, originality, flexibility, and authenticity of the goal; the second level is the ability of the applicant to overcome the obstacle to achieving the goal. The third level is the ability to independently define goals in the process of self-improvement.

C. Mouran[83] considers activity as an active interaction of a person with the environment, in the process of which consciously set goals are achieved and realized. Activity and communication are interpreted in two interconnected ways. Secondly, communication - joint activity, the exchange of collected information, mutual attitude, the identification of another person and the development of a clear strategy of change - will allow us to agree on a variety of, multifaceted tasks that arise from the need. In relation to the didactics of the English language, it is separately defined as "the phenomenon of interactive information exchange between two or more optical persons, who are considered to have a social status, and who work or write in their turn on a piece of text or a written text."

Communication can be both the mediator of activity and the activity itself. In the philosophical lexicon, in Latin, communike is interpreted as giving advice, news, communication, writing, communication, exchange of opinion, information. In psychological literature, the term "relation" is interpreted as "the mutual ratio of two or more optical persons in the exchange of information about mutual cognition, mutual dependence. "Communication " is interpreted in terms of "mutual relations," "relationship" or "personal work." "Communication is one of the forms of self-assessment of a person, representing one of the forms of a person who cries."

" Communication is a meaningful communication." If a person changes the process, taking into account the approaching action schedule of the person, they will receive the information. By the way." According to L.C. Vygotsky, human opinion never corresponds to the literal meaning of a word. Therefore, when communicating, personality should be different, and in the case of oral speech, it is important to understand the process of communication, not only lexical and syntactic, but also syntactic.

The formation of competencies takes place over a period of 30-40 years of personality development, during which students study at a higher educational institution and actively engage in professional activities. The foundation of the educational process is laid during the period of study in a higher educational institution. The content of the process of forming responsibility is the stage of elevating it to the level of individuality and socialization. A new achievement for individuality is the success of forming a leading motivating young person in higher education and the subsequent activity of their profession.

Individuality is a managerial function related to the development of professional opportunities. Responsibility is defined as the ability of each individual to form and transfer to another state of activity, to carry out self-assessment, to develop educational and professional activity, to create a system of effective methods for achieving the goals of achieving the goal of developing an individual's activity, to develop motivation.

For this reason, the main topic of our research was formed as follows: the foreign demand for professional competence is formed internally and externally by the person and is mastered. In order to self-adjust and improve the process of mastering native language, skills, and abilities, it is an individual experience and reflection that is renewed in process for professional and personal development. Culture includes other forms of communication.

CONCLUSIONS

1. It is important to develop knowledge and operational-technological skills in the motivational, moral, social, and behavioral spheres of future engineers based on a competency-based approach. In this case, competence should include the following components: a) readiness to demonstrate competence, which is considered as the mobilization of subjective forces (motivational); b) mastery of knowledge about the content of competencies (cognitive); c) experience of competence in various situations (behavior); d) content of competence and its object of application (value); e) emotional-volitional regulation of the process and demonstration of competence; f) the ability to demonstrate competence in various situations.

2. The emphasis on developing

competencies based on English language learning is intended to shift from the educational and scientific side of education to the content side (without sacrificing their value) and to the expected results. In this case, it is necessary to develop personal professional abilities that meet the requirements of the stimulating labor market, along with the correspondence of the training provided to the future specialist to the requirements set;

3. The three criteria for future English language proficiency are the setting of these goals: the first level of goals, their novelty, originality, adaptability, stability, validity, and realism; the second level is the ability of students to overcome obstacles in their achievements by correcting them. The third level is the ability to independently set goals in the process of self-education.

4. The methodological model for

developing communicative competence based on integrated English language instruction for future engineers, developed by us, implies the sequential development of communicative competence, with the linguistic block becoming more invariant. Interdisciplinary integration of English with engineering subjects contributed to the development of professional cognitive abilities in the exchange of student motives, as well as communicative orientation and professional orientation;

5. The theoretical core, conceptual models, hypotheses, postulates, main content, and functional content are the foundation of integrative teaching of engineering disciplines in English. Integrative classes were bilingual, and the presentation of the teaching material was conducted in a blend: in English and in the native language. It is justified that the communicative competence of future engineers based on English

language instruction should be implemented through the effective use of teaching methods, the development of methodological support, and the provision of interdisciplinary integration.

6. The effectiveness of improving the communicative competence of future engineers based on English language learning has been proven through experimental work. In the process of organizing independent work in general professional and specialized subjects based on integrative methods of teaching English, methodological manuals have been developed that include the development of communicative competence among students.

7. It has been established that students have developed communicative competence as a result of their understanding of English in a professional sense. The coefficient of communicative competence development based on English language instruction for students in the

experimental group was consistently higher than in the control groups, and according to the results of the pedagogical experiment, the methodology developed by us proved to be effective.

Scientific and methodological recommendations for improving the methodology of improving the communicative competence of engineering students based on English language teaching:

1. Development of methodological recommendations and teaching materials for the development of communicative competence of engineering students based on an integrative approach.
2. Organizing the effective use of software tools for the methodology of developing engineering knowledge among students in technical universities.

USED LITERATURE

I. Normative documents, political literature:

1. Ўзбекистон Республикасининг 2020 йил 23 сентябрдаги "Таълим тўғрисида"ги ЎРҚ-637-сон Қонуни. https://lex.uz/docs/5013007

2. Ўзбекистон Республикаси Президентининг 2012 йил 10 декабрдаги "Чет тилларни ўрганиш тизимини янада такомиллаштириш чора-тадбирлари тўғрисида"ги ПҚ-1875-сонли Қарори. https://lex.uz/docs/2126032

3. Ўзбекистон Республикаси Президентининг 2017 йил 7 февралдаги "Ўзбекистон Республикасини янада ривожлантириш бўйича Ҳаракатлар Стратегияси тўғрисида"ги ПФ-4947-сон Фармони. https://lex.uz/docs/3107036

4. Ўзбекистон Республикаси

Президентининг 2018 йил 5 июндаги ПҚ-3775-сонли "Олий таълим муассасаларида таълим сифатини ошириш ва уларнинг мамлакатда амалга оширилаётган кенг қамровли ислоҳотларда фаол иштирокини таъминлаш бўйича қўшимча чора-тадбирлар тўғрисида"ги қарори.

II. Monograph, scientific article, patent, scientific collections

5. Агаркова Е.И. Моделирование системы повышения профессио-нально-педагогической компетентности специалиста в условиях ИПКРО : дис. ... канд. пед. наук:. – Тамбов, 2004. – 238 с.

6. Ахрарова Ф.Б. Нофилологик олий ўқув юртлари талабаларига чет тилларини ўқитишда педагогик технологиялардан фойдаланиш методикаси. Пед.ф.ф.док.(PhD) дисс.автореф. -Т.2021. – 52 б.

7. Ахмедова Л.Т., Нормуратова В.И. Teaching English Practicum. Практикум по методике преподавания английского языка. – Ташкент, 2011.

8. Ашуров А.А.Техника олий таълим муассасалари бакалавр талабалари коммуникатив инглиз тили компетенциясининг шаклланишида шахсга йўналтирилган ёндашув. Пед.ф.ф.док.(PhD) дисс.автореф. -Т.2020.- 49 б.

9. Байденко В.И. Компетенции в профессиональном образовании (к освоению компетентностного подхода) // Высшее образование в России. – М.: 2004. – №11. – С. 3-13.

10. Бакиева Г.Х., Ирискулов М.Т., Ким Н.Н. English for Professional Development. – Ташкент, 2011.

11. Безукладников К.Э. Формирование лингводидактических компетенций будущего

учителя иностранного языка: концепция и методика: дис. д-ра пед.наук: – Н. Новгород, 2009. – 403 с.

12. Белозерцев Е.П., Гонеев А.Д., Пашков А.Г. и др. Педагогика профессионального образования: Учеб. пособие для студ. высш. пед. учеб. заведений / Под ред. В. А. Сластенина. - М.: Издательский центр «Академия», 2006. - 368 с.

13. Берулава М.Н. Интеграция содержания образования. - М.: Изд-во «Совершенство», 1998.

14. Бим И.Л. Концепция обучения второму иностранному языку (немецкий на базе английского): Учеб. пособие. Обнинск: Титул, 2001, 45 с.

15. Болонский процесс: середина пути / под науч. ред. д-ра пед. наук, проф. В.И. Байденко. – М.: Исслед. центр проблем качества подготовки специалистов; Рос. Новый ун-т,

2005. – 379 с.

16. Бондаревская Е.В. Научно-теоретические основы личностно-ориентированного образования//Личностно-ориентированный образовательный процесс: сущность, содержание, технологии / под ред. Е.В. Бондаревской. – Ростов н/Д, 1995.

17. Бонк Н.А., Лукьянова Н.А., Памухина Л.Г. Учебник английского языка. -М., 1995.- 637с.

18. Борисов Ю.Б. К проблеме листа и роли литературного текста в обучении иностранному языку в языковом вузе // Методика обучения иностранным языкам. – Минск, 1986. – Вып. I.

19. Буланова-Топоркова М.В. Педагогика и психология высшей школы: Учеб. пособие. – Ростов н/Д : Феникс, 2002. – 544 с.

20. Вербицкий А.А., Ларионова О.Г. Личностный и компетентностный подходы в

образовании: проблемы интеграции. - М.: Логос, 2009. - 336 с.

21. Воспитательная деятельность педагога: Учеб. пособие для студентов высш. Учеб. заведений / И. А. Колесникова [и др.]; под общ. ред. В.А. Сластёнина и И.А. Колесниковой. – 3-е изд., стер. – М.: Академия, 2007.

22. Возможные подходы к проектированию ГОС ВПО 3-го поколения и нового Перечня для направлений (специальностей) классического университетского образования / Группа экспертов YMO по классическому университетскому образованию.

23. Выготский Л.С. Педагогическая психология. М., 2005.

24. Гавриленко Н.Н. Теория и методика обучения переводу в сфере профессиональной коммуникации. Кн. 1. – М.: 2009.

25. Гальскова Н.Д., Гез Н.И. Теория

обучения иностранным языкам. Лингводидактика и методика: Учеб. пособие для студентов лингв. ун-тов и фак. ин. яз. высш. пед. учеб. заведений. –4-е изд. –М.: Академия, 2007. – 336 с.

26. Галямина И.Г. Проектирование государственных образовательных стандартов высшего профессионального образования нового поколения с использованием компетентностного подхода: матлы к шестому заседанию методологического семинара 29 марта 2005 года. – М.: Исслед. центр проблем качества подготовки специалистов, 2005.

27. Гез Н.И. Формирование коммуникативной компитенции как объект зарубежных исследований. ИЯШ, 1985, № 2, С. 17-22.

28. Герменевтика: проблемы исследования понимания // Вопросы методологии. – 1994. – № 1–2.

29. Грицанов, А.А., Можейко М.А. Постмодернизм: энцикл. / – М.: Интерпрессервис, 2001.

30. Гурвич П.Б. Обучение иностранным языкам: поиск новых путей // ИЯШ. – 1988. – № 3. – С. 7–8.

31. Дидактика средней школы / под ред. М. Н. Скаткина, И.Я. Лернера. – М., 1975.

32. Джураев Р.Х. Таълимда интерфаол технологиялар.–Т., 2010.- 87 б.

33. Долгушина Т.Н. Развитие иноязычного потенциала студентов технического университета: дис. ... канд. пед. наук. – Магнитогорск, 2003. – 187 с.

34. Жалолов Ж.Ж Чет тил укитиш методикаси. Олий ўкув юртлари талабалари учун дарслик. –Ўқтувчи.Ташкент, 1996.

35. Жалолов Ж.Ж. Чет тили ўқитиш методикаси. –Тошкент, 2012.

36. Зимняя И.А. Компетентность человека -

новое качество результата образования // Материалы XIII Всероссийского совещания «Проблемы качества образования». Книга 2. - М.: Исследовательский центр проблем качества подготовки специалистов, 2003. - С. 4-15

37. Зимняя И.А. Педагогическая психология. – Ростов н/Д, 1997.

38. Зимняя, И. А. Ключевые компетентности – новая парадигма результата образования // Высшее образование сегодня. – 2003. – № 5. – С. 35.

39. Иванова С.П. Личностно-ориентированное обучение как фактор повышения качества знаний у студентов технических факультетов университета (на примере иностранного языка): дис. ... канд. пед. наук. – Курган, 2003. – 167 с.

40. Игна О.Н. Развитие социокультурной компетенции студентов на основе

аутентичных материалов при профессионально-ориентированном обучении иноязычному общению (немецкий язык, технический вуз): дис. ... канд. пед. наук:. – Томск, 2003. – 186 с.

41. Илхамова И.Н.Нофилологик таълим йўналишидаги талабаларнинг ижтимоий-маданий компетентлиги контекстида нутқ кўникмаларини такомиллаштириш. Пед.ф.ф.док.(PhD) дисс.автореф. -Т.2020. -46 б.

42. Иностранные языки в высшей школе: сб. науч.-метод. ст. / под ред. С.К. Фоломкиной. – Вып. 24. – М.: Изд-во МПИ, 1991. – 159 с.

43. Иноятов У.И, Б.Ходжаев. "Умумтаълимий компетецияларни лойиҳалаштиришнинг концептуал асослари". Халқ таълими журнали. 2016. 2-сон. 8 бет.

44. Исмоилова З.К. Талабаларнинг касбий педагогик малакаларини шакллантириш.:

Автореф. дис. ... пед. фан. ном. – Т.: 2000. – 186 б.

45. Исроилова Д.М. Нофилологик олий ўқув юртларида талабаларни фанлараро боғлиқликда касбга йўналтирилган инглиз тилига ўқитиш (технология факультети мисолида). Пед.ф.ф.док.(PhD) дисс.автореф. -Т.2020.-58 б.

46. Кадирова М.Р. Тилларга ихтисослашмаган олий таълим муассасалари талабаларига инглиз тилини ўргатишда ижодий фаолликни модернизациялаш. Пед.ф.ф.док.(PhD) дисс.автореф. -Т.2018.-46 б.

47. Караулов Ю.Н. Русский язык и языковая личность. – М., 1987.

48. Ковальчук М.А. Дискуссия как средство обучения иноязычному общению: метод. пособие для преподавателей иностранных языков. –М.: Высш. шк. науч.-образовательный центр «Школа

Китайгородской», 2008.

49. Коммуникация // Философский энциклопедический словарь. – М.: ИНФРА-М, 1999. – С. 145.

50. Коммуникация // Словарь практического психолога. – Минск, 1997. – С. 191.

51. Кон И.С. Психология ранней юности: Книга для учителя. – М.: Просвещение, 1989. – 255 с.

52. Корочкина М.Г. Формирование межкультурной компетенции в техническом университете (Английский язык): дис. ... канд. пед. наук:. –Таганрог, 2000. – 178 с.

53. Коряковцева Н.Ф. Современная методика организации самостоятельной работы изучающих иностранный язык. – М., 2002. – 77 с.

54. Костриков О.И. Методика проектирования дистанционного обучения студентов вузов физической культуры и

педагогические критерии его эффективности: дис. ... канд. пед. наук. – Малаховка, 2003. – 175 с.

55. Кравченко А. И. Психология и педагогика: учебник. – М.: Проспект, 2009.

56. Крылов, Эдуард Геннадьевич Интегративное билингвальное обучение иностранному языку и инженерным дисциплинам в техническом вузе : диссертация ... доктора педагогических наук : 13.00.02 Екатеринбург 2016

57. Кузнецова Р.А. Дидактические условия реализации гуманистической направленности инженерно-педагогического образования в педагогическом вузе: дис. ... канд. пед. наук. – Волгоград, 1996. – 185 с.

58. Кузьмина Н.В. Профессионализм личности преподавателя и мастера производственного обучения. - М., 1990.

59. Кумбс Ф.Г. Кризис образования в

современном мире. Системный анализ. – М., 1970.

60. Лапидус Б.А. Интенсификация процесса обучения иноязычной речи // ИЯШ. – 1988. – № 3. – С. 7–8.

61. Леонтьева В. Гуманистические перспективы образования // Высшее образование в России. – 1994. – № 4.

62. Леушина И.В. Совершенствование иноязычной подготовки будущих специалистов технического профиля в условиях многоуровневой системы высшего профессионального образования: дис. ... канд. пед. наук:. – Н. Новгород, 2003. – 221 с.

63. Мазаева И.А., Зимняя И.А., Лаптева М.Д., Морозова Н.А. Инновационно-компетентностная образовательная программа по учебной дисциплине: опыт проектирования / Под научн. ред. д. психол. н., проф., акад. РАО И.А. Зимней. - М., М: Исследовательский

центр проблем качества подготовки специалистов, 2008. – 122 стр.

64. Маматкулов Х.А. Хорижий тиллар бўйича ҳарбий педагоглар касбий компетентлигини ривожлантиришнинг илмий-услубий асосларини такомиллаштириш. Пед.фан.док.(DSc) дисс.автореф. -Т.2021.-54 б

65. Маткова М.В. Совершенствование подготовки операторов информационных систем военного назначения иноязычному профессиональному взаимодействию (на примере подготовки специалистов в области ядерной безопасности): дис. ... канд. пед. наук. – М., 2002. – 164 с.

66. Махкамова Г.Т. Концепция формирования межкультурной компетенции студентов факультетов английского языка. – Ташкент, 2010. – 208 с.

67. Махкамова М.У.Техника олий таълим муассасаларининг ўқув жараёнида

талабаларда ахборот маданиятини шакллантириш. Пед.ф.ф.док.(PhD) дисс.автореф. -Т.2019.-48 б.

68. Межуева И.Е. Развитие творческой активности студентов неязыкового вуза в процессе моделирования иноязычной профессиональной деятельности будущего специалиста: дис. ... канд. пед. наук:. – Тула, 2004. – 231 с.

69. Меркулова Л.П. Формирование профессиональной мобильности специалистов технического профиля средствами иностранного языка: дис…д-ра пед. наук.- Самара, 2008. — 455с.

70. Методика обучения иностранным языкам в средней школе: учебник / Н.И. Гез [и др.]. – М.: Высш. шк., 1982. – С. 45.

71. Методика преподавания иностранных языков в высшей школе / под ред. С.Г. Тер-Минасовой. – М.: Изд-во МГУ, 1993. – 136 с.

72. Муслимов Н.А. "Бўлажак касб таълими ўқитувчиларини касбий шакллантириш. Монография. - Т.: Фан, 2004 - 126 б.

73. Муслимов Н.А. Касб таълими ўқитувчисини касбий шакллантиришнинг назарий-методик асослари: Пед.фан. док. ... дис. Автореф. Ташкент: ТДПУ, 2007.-47 б.

74. Мухитдинова М.Р. Умумий ўрта таълим мактаби битирувчиларини инглиз тилига масофавий ўқитишнинг усул ва воситалари. Пед.ф.ф.док.(PhD) дисс.автореф. -Т.2020.-52 б.

75. Немирович О. В. Изучение иностранных языков как средство гуманитаризации высшего технического образования. Дис. канд.пед.наук. Москва, 1999. -175с.

76. Никанорова И.Я. Особенности использования системно-структурного критерия в определении профессиональной компетентности учителя: дис. ... канд. пед. наук: – Комсомольск-на-Амуре, 2003. – 192 с.

77. Нурманов А.Т. Талабаларни самарали мулоқот технологияси ва техникасига тайёрлашнинг педагогик имкониятлари (аудиториядан ташқари машғулотлар мисолида). Пед.фан.док.(DSc) дисс.автореф. - Т.2017.-87 б.

78. Пассов Е.И. Урок иностранного языка в средней школе. –М.: Просвещение 1988. – 223 с.

79. Патарая Е.С. Модернизация содержания профессионально-ориентированного обучения студентов неязыковых вузов / Традиции и инновации в методике обучения иностранным языкам. – СПб. : КАРО, 2007.

80. Пашков А.Г., Гонеев А.Д. Педагогические основы социальной реабилитации детей с ограниченными возможностями. Курск: Изд-во КГМУ, 1999. 234 с.

81. Педагогика профессионального

образования: учеб. пособие для студентов высш. учеб. заведений / Е. П. Белозерцев [и др.]; под ред. В.А. Сластёнина. – 3-е изд., стер. – М.: Академия, 2007.

82. Петрулева Р., Дулина Н., Токарев В. О главной цели образования / Высшее образование в России. – 1998. – № 3.

83. Пищулин В.Г. Модель выпускника университета / Педагогика. – 2002. – № 9.

84. Платон. Диалоги. – М.: Мысль, 1998. – 528 с.

85. Примов Ш.Қ. Бўлажак ўқитувчиларнинг коммуникатив компетентлигини ривожлантириш. Пед.ф.ф.док.(PhD) дисс.автореф. -Т.2020.-42 б.

86. Рац М. Школа гуманитарной инженерии. Концептуальный проект / http://www.geocities.ws/anatoly_49447/Z02Rus.htm

87. Ойзерман М.Т. Размышления об

инновациях // Вопросы методологии, 1991. - №1.-С.8-19.

88. Равен Дж. Педагогическое тестирование: проблемы, заблуждения, перспективы / Дж. Равен. 2-е изд., испр. - М.: Когито - Центр, - 2001. - 139 с.

89. Равен Джон. Компетентность в современном обществе. Выявление, развитие и реализация. - М., 2002.

90. Рискулова К.Д. Бўлажак инглиз тили ўқитувчилари социолингвистик компетентлигини шакллантириш тизими. Пед.фан.док.(DSc) дисс.автореф. -Т.2017.-62 б.

91. Рогова Г.В., Рабинович Ф.М., Сахарова Т.Е. Методика обучения иностранным языкам в средней школе. – М.: Просвещение, 1991.

92. Рогулина Е.В. Взаимодействие психологических механизмов стереотипизации и рефлексии как условие развития профессиональной компетентности

учителя: дис. канд. психол. наук. –Череповец, 2000. – 177 с.

93. Русско-английский словарь научно-технической лексики, около 30000 слов и словосочетаний, Кузнецов Б.В., 1992.

94. Соловова Е.Н. Методика обучения иностранным языкам: продвинутый курс: пособие для студентов и учителей – 2-е изд. – М.: АСТ : Астрель, 2010. – 272 с.

95. Соловова, Е. Н. Методика обучения иностранным языкам: базовый курс лекций: пособие для студентов и учителей. – 4-е изд. – М.: Просвещение, 2006. – 239 с.

96. Семёнова М.Ю. Основы перевода текста: учебник. Ростов н/Д: Феникс, 2009. 343 с.

97. Серова Т. С., Шишкина Л. П. Иноязычный экологический лексикон тезаурусного типа как средство формирования категориально-понятийного аппарата будущих

специалистов // Сибирский педагогический журнал. 2010. №2

98. Сиромясов О.В. Формирование межкультурной профессиональной компетенции специалиста на основе иноязычного текста: Немецкий язык, неязыковой вуз. Дисс. кандидат педагогических наук.2000.

99. Сластёнин В.А. Отчетный доклад президента МАНПО // Педагогическое образование и наука. – М., 2005.

100. Смирнов С.Д. Педагогика и психология высшего образования: от деятельности к личности. – М.: Аспект-Пресс, 1995.

101. Современный словарь иностранных слов: ок. 20 000 слов. – 2-е изд., стер. – М.: Рус. яз., 1999.

102. Соловова Е.Н. Методика обучения иностранным языкам: базовый курс: пособие для студентов и учителей. – 2-е изд. – М.:

АСТ: Астрель, 2008.

103. Соловова Е.Н. Методика обучения иностранным языкам: продвинутый курс: пособие для студентов и учителей. –2-е изд. – М.: АСТ: Астрель, 2010. – 272 с.

104. Степень бакалавра: что это такое ?: мат-лы междунар. семинара, 25–26 нояб. 2004 г. – СПб., 2004.

105. Тайсаева С.Б. Взаимодействие значимости работы и ценностных ориентаций при выборе и реализации профессионального пути: дис. ... канд. психол. наук. – М., 1999. – 173 с.

106. Тард Г. Социальная логика. – СпБ.: Ленанд, 2020. – 504 с.

107. Татур Ю.Г. Компетентность в структуре модели качества подготовки специалистов // Высшее образование сегодня. – 2004. – № 3.

108. Теоретические основы методики обучения иностранным языкам в средней

школе / под ред. А.Д. Климентенко, А.А. Миролюбова. – М.: Педагогика, 1981.

109. Умарова Я.Т. Тил таълимида матн таҳлили орқали ўқувчиларда прагматик компетенцияни ривожлантириш. Пед.ф.ф.док.(PhD) дисс.автореф. -Наманган. 2020.-53 б.

110. Фадейкина О.В. Формирование иноязычной коммуникативной компетентности будущих офицеров: дис. ... канд. пед. наук. – Екатеринбург, 2001. – 182 с.

111. Философский энциклопедический словарь. – М.: ИНФРА-М, 1999.

112. Фоломкина С.К. Типовая программа по иностранным языкам/ – М., 1991. – 65 с.

113. Ходурская В.А. Пособие по английскому языку для математических факультетов университетов. Учебное пособие. English for students of Mathematics: М. Высшая школа. 1975 г. 175 с.

114. Хомский Н. Язык и проблемы знания. - Благовещенск, БГК им. А.И. Бодуэна де Куртене. 1999. 252 с.

115. Хуторской А.В. Методика личностно-ориентированного обучения. Как обучать всех по разному ? - М.:ВЛАДОС-ПРЕСС.2005.

116. Шаропова Ш.Қ., ва бошқа. Factors for developing the professional compe-tence of professional teachers. International Journal of Psychosocial Rehabilitation, Vol. 24, Issue 04, 2020 ISSN: 1475-7192, pp 6839-6845.

117. Шаропова Ш.Қ., ва бошқа. The Method of Creative Learning of Higher Edu-cation Institute's Teachers in the Courses of Advanced Training and Retraining of Staff. PSYCHOLOGY AND EDUCATION (2021) 58(2): 1295-1305 ISSN: 00333077.

118. Шаропова Ш.Қ. Interdisciplinary Interaction as Basis of Forming Integrative Competencies of University Students. Eastern

European Scientific Journal (ISSN 2199-7977), Germany 2018, 184-189.

119. Шаропова Ш.Қ. Развитие системы профессионально-ориентированного обучения иностранным языкам в техническом вузе на основе предметно-языковой интеграции. «Школа Будущего», № 4, 2018, ст-123-130.

120. Шаропова Ш.Қ. Study of a foreign language in a technical university in the system of humanities edu-cation. ACADEMICIA: An International Multidisciplinary Research Journal ISSN: 2249-7137 Vol. 11 Issue 1, January 2021 Impact Factor: SJIF 2021 = 7.492

121. Шаропова Ш.Қ., Химматалиев Д.О. Professional Development Of A Teacher Of Foreign Languages - Electronic Educational Resources. The American Journal of Social Science and Education In-novations. (ISSN – 2689-100x) IMPACT FACTOR Published: January 25, 2021 | Pages: 191-194.

122. Шаропова Ш.Қ. Формирование профессиональной компетенции у студентов неязыкового ВУЗа. «Муғаллим ҳәм узликсиз Билимлетдириў»,№4 Нөкис, 2019. – 11-14-бетлар.

123. Щедровицкий Г.П. Психология и методология (1): Ситуация и условия возникновения концепции поэтапного формирования умственных действий (из архива Г.П. Щедровицкого). – М.: Путь, 2004. – Т. 2. – Вып. 1.

124. Шумпетер Й. Теория экономического развития (Исследование предпринимательской прибыли, капитала, кредита, процента и цикла конъюнктуры) /; пер. с англ. – М.: Прогресс, 1982. – 455 с.

125. Языковое образование в вузе: метод. пособие для преподавателей высшей школы, аспирантов и студентов. – СПб.: КАРО, 2005.

III. Other used literature

126. Blunkett, D. Modernising Higher Education – Fasing the Global Challenge / D. Blunkett. – N.Y.: Department for Education and Employment, 2000. – 45 p.

127. Engineering Accreditation Criteria. www.abet.org/forms.shtml
http://www.abet.org/forms.shtml

128. Ek J. van. Coping. The Language Teacher. – 1988. – № 1/1.

129. English dictionary for advanced learners. – L.: Macmillan, 2002.

130. Descy, P. Training and learning for competence / P. Descy, M. Tessaring. – Luxembourg: Office for Official Publication of the European Communities, 2001.

131. Jones R.H. Creativity in Language Teaching: Perspectives from Research and Practice. – New York: Routledge, 1992. - 284 p.

132. Krashen, Stephen. Some issues relating to the monitor model // Teaching and learning

English as a Second Language: Trends in Research and Practice: On TESOL 77: Selected Papers from the Eleventh Annual Convention of Teachers of English to Speakers of Other Languages, Miami, Florida, April 26 – May 1, 1987

133. L. Malvern. Introduction to the Mechanics of a Continuous Medium. 711 p

134. Manfred Tessaring. Training for a changing society: A report on current vocational education and training research in Europe (Reference document) Paperback – January 1, 1998. 294 p.

135. Moirand, Sophie. Enseigner a communiquer en langues etrangere. Hachette, 1990. 188 p. (Моуран С)

136. https://tashkent.hh.uz/

137. White, R.W. Motivation reconsidered: The concept of competence // Psychological review. – 1959. – №66. – p.38-54.

www.ingramcontent.com/pod-product-compliance
Lightning Source LLC
LaVergne TN
LVHW021222080526
838199LV00089B/5785